C000153308

phrases, of which it takes two (or eight bars) to complete the pattern. Each of the two voices has a compass of over five octaves; and here is the first four-bar half-limb of the sequence in the leading voice:

Meanwhile the other voice is vibrating, filling in the harmony, and finding its way down to C, which it reaches at b.83, and there proceeds to answer the first voice. The obvious division between r. and l. also contributes its meaning, and is in Beethoven's mind at the step 88–89. The nuances in brackets in the present edition are, of course, not Beethoven's, but they make this sense clear. As to the quintoles, Beethoven selected so strange a group just because it obliterates the quaver beats while descending the necessary distance. Accentuating the main beats not only marks the obvious and unimportant, but draws attention to the steps in which this unimportant pattern does not fit (e.g., the ends of 83, 84, where it must do goose-step, and 87). In bb.91–92 the alternation between A♭ and A♮ must be clearly marked.

b.125 The suggestion to take r.h. a third higher in the last group (so as to reach the D♭ which was not on Beethoven's pianoforte) is mistaken. This compressed group is the sole origin of the brilliant repercussion between the hands which persists during the next four bars. Moreover, the climax is in the D♭ of l.h. at the beginning of 126; and this must not be forestalled.

But the whole passage (123–134) is ruined by three traditional abuses. First there is the commonplace habit of accentuating the steps of the arpeggios. Many commentators who have noticed the rising bass of bb.109–123 proceed to show that it means nothing to them by remarking with equal enthusiasm that Beethoven descends for two octaves on a chord of the diminished seventh. This is like pointing out the exact cost of the damage done to princely garments in the calamities of the last act of *Hamlet*.

The point of bb.123–131 lies in Beethoven's pedal mark. He wishes the whole pianoforte to be filled with the chord. An even *fortissimo*, unpricked (and therefore undeflated) by accents, accumulates power through the unchanging pedal. When Beethoven and Mendelssohn (who follows him closely in this matter) say *sempre Ped.*, they mean not merely 'always with pedal', but precisely 'with unchanged pedal'. The modern pianoforte here realises Beethoven's purpose as he might have enjoyed it in dreams. We might even venture to extend it by continuing the pedal through 132–133. The blur would be Beethovenish; he prescribes it himself in bb.235–237. But all this is frustrated by another traditional abuse.

Already in Bülow's day the custom arose of adding octaves to l.h. at 130–133. The player who is not excited in this passage – that is to say, who is not stimulated to the tensest self-control in the ambition to communicate its emotion to the listener – should give up music altogether. But it needs no brains to make a big noise, and the noise of this passage with octaves is bigger than anything Beet-

hoven ever conceived [...] artist to make a clima[...] nothing of the kind. It has no ring in the treble and no articulation in the bass. Its colour is sooty, dull and wrong: wrong as the colour of the climax in the first movement of the C minor symphony would be wrong if the main parts were doubled in octaves.

Even this is not the worst. Beethoven writes a sudden *piano* at 134. It is not difficult to make clear; it needs practice, but can be achieved without a comma or any other affected gesture. The vainest of 'star' conductors would not risk his reputation by shirking so characteristic a nuance in Beethoven's most reckless orchestration. The 'pianistic' standards are unfortunately lower. Bülow suppresses the *p* and with a twinge of conscience uses small print for the *f* which he substitutes. Edition Steingräber has the *piano*, but precedes it by ⎯⎯ . Herr G. Damm's copious comments on the peculiarities of autographs and the errors of other editions do not include a hint that this *diminuendo* is spurious. Such an editor pronounces his own condemnation.

bb.204–209 There is no excuse for the corruption that has often crept into the text here. According to the corrupt version, the entire first half of b.204 is thrice repeated in the r.h., and so also with the first half of b.206. The mistake is said to come from 'misunderstanding Beethoven's abbreviation marks'. But these are exactly what it is impossible to misunderstand; and they are a real help to the eye. Accordingly, they are given here at the end of these notes, so that the reader can see how indisputable the text is.

b.235 Note that the *piano* at 235 is sudden. This needs some management of Beethoven's very necessary pedal, otherwise neither the *piano* nor the rhythmic figure will be clear enough. But, as has already been remarked, Beethoven intends the figure to emerge out of a blur. Having understood his meaning, it is for you to induce your pianoforte to express it. No two instruments will react in quite the same way, except perhaps at the sudden cold daylight when the pedal ceases in the middle of b.237.

Più allegro
Get a sharp rhythm at this crash: nothing is more futile than an 'agogic accent', as if you were shrugging your shoulders or playing a ruminating string of epigrams. Announce a steady and markedly faster tempo, and stick to it.

Bars 248–249 See that the first figure of b.249 sounds like a development of the previous cadence. Do not use a *martellatto* (or 'hammered') touch, but let the chords fall from the height of your wrist without taking your fingertips off the keys. As the bass becomes lower, do not let it overpower the r.h. In bb.251, 254 and 255 play twelve equal chords, not a set of spiky accents. Make your climax by an increase in the use of pedal, used only for the *sf* chords until b.255, and then on each beat. Do not be afraid of Beethoven's final pedal. Release it only after four normal beats in b.262 and then let the ghost of the written chord reverberate by itself in the pause.

Andante con moto

It is no easy task to play this theme and variations accurately; and without accuracy we shall never realise its solemnity. Until the third variation, Beethoven's marks and notation can be taken as covering the whole ground. We know the difference between dots and double dots; and if we doubt the advice that the quaver chords of the first variation should suggest soft trombones, we need only play exact quavers with good balance of tone in order to understand how soft trombones might sound. (A large part of the beauty of orchestral colouring consists in the fact that orchestral players are trained to meticulous accuracy.) A sensitive artist will not be tempted to stress the obvious by 'bringing out the melody' in the second variation. Those arpeggios are enjoying their own rise and fall across the rhythm, and the player of any other instrument than the pianoforte would enjoy them for their own sake. The fact that they also trace the main theme is obvious enough without pulling them this way and that to show it. In the third variation Beethoven's marking is not complete. We may take it that *dolce* and *forte* are regarded by him as contradictory, so that on the word *dolce* some decline must be made from a previous *forte*.

On this assumption our bracketed marks of expression complete a scheme indicated by Beethoven by his *fortes* in bb.54/55 & 62/63 taken in connection with the *dolce* in b.72. It is practically certain that Beethoven intends to alternate pairs of relatively soft bars with pairs of *forte* bars, the *sforzandos* not destroying the *piano* or *mezzo piano* represented by *dolce*, while the *fortes* are steady, and not punctured by *sforzandos*. At all events this is a dignified scheme, and Beethoven has gone far to indicate that such is his intention.

Bars 96–97 It would be incredible, if the facts were not self-evident, that the perfectly clear indication in Beethoven's autograph at b.97 has been unintelligibly misprinted in all but the most modern editions. After indicating an unbroken arpeggio sign for the whole chord in b.96, Beethoven indicates an arpeggiated l.h. chord and an unbroken r.h. chord in b.97. To remove all possible doubt he writes the word *arpeggio* under the l.h. chord, and the word *secco* (i.e., 'dry'; sc. 'unbroken') under the r.h. chord. The word *arpeggio* has been carefully preserved in most editions, but the word *secco* has been omitted for a century. Nothing can be more unintelligible than the word *arpeggio* by itself. It has given rise to the wildest conjectures; for no other kind of conjecture is possible. Now try Beethoven's device. Do not change the pedal. And do not force the tone: an engine-whistle is more powerful than a human shriek, but it is far less dramatic. You will find that Beethoven gives exactly the right method for producing the equivalent of a human shriek, far better than the device of singling out the top note for the left hand. Spread the l.h. arpeggio quite wide and, relying on the pedal, do not waste finger-power in holding the notes down. Put the unbroken r.h. chord on (or a little before) the top note of l.h. Hold the chord for quite a long pause, but do not let a silence intervene between it and the Allegro.

* *A Companion to Beethoven's Pianoforte Sonatas: A Complete Book of Analyses.* (Associated Board)

Allegro ma non troppo

This movement is often taken too fast. Beethoven is rather sparing of the warning *ma non troppo*, and it occurs oftener in later than in earlier works. It is therefore not a warning that should be neglected.

Bar 14 Count in two-bar periods from here to 19.

b.20 Bülow's excellent if unorthodox fingering ⌐1 2 4 3 4 3 2 | 1 4 3 2 1 3 4 2 | brings this theme at all tone-values within the grasp of a small hand, and ensures an accent on the second beat ranging from the normal clearness needed in *pp* to the powerful *sf* indicated by Beethoven in *forte* developments. The fingering ⌐1 2 3 4 5, etc., is not so difficult as it is found to be by players who will not carry their hand, but insist on leaving the thumb in its note. In any case it is well to bring the thumb on to the A♭ at the beginning of the second bar.

bb.36 ff. It has become a tradition to give a hard *sforzando* to every pair of repeated notes (♩ | ♩) in bb.36–37, and the other places where Beethoven has omitted it. This custom is perhaps due not merely to perversity, but has a certain traditional basis in Czerny's statement that a *sforzando* in such repeated notes is inevitable. But this will certainly not do for Beethoven, to whom such difficulties are merely provocative of the command to overcome them. He so little agrees with Czerny's plea that within a year of this sonata he is demanding the nuance (♩ | ♩ below f, p) in repeated l.h. chords at full speed in the finale of the E♭ Trio, Op.70 No.2. All the evidence confirms the view that the mood of bb.36–63 is not hard, but lyric in a profound melancholy, as fits so enormous an expanse in which there is no action. It is nearly as long as the whole second group. (See analysis in *A Companion to Beethoven's Pianoforte Sonatas.**)

bb.76–80 It is no oversight that bb.76 & 78 end with D♭, while b.80 ends with D♮. This point is a touchstone for your sense of key.

b.118 It is interesting to find Beethoven so anxious to have the second part of this movement repeated (contrary to all precedent when the first was not) that he actually gives this explicit direction in the autograph. One good effect of the repeat would be that the episode, bb.142–157, would gain a certain symmetry by thus recurring. A more important point is that in the Coda the new *presto* theme would gain enormously by having been delayed. These things Beethoven imagined vividly; what he overlooked was the enormous emotional power of the collapse and slow return in bb.176–210, a passage as impossible to go through twice as the death of a hero. It is interesting that he overlooks what everybody finds easy to praise and attaches importance to what nobody can see until it is proved by experience. We may think him wrong; but his error is anything but conventional.

b.135 The autograph is quite clear in giving a broad swell to this lower part. The accents and the *crescendos* were probably added in the proof-sheets. The passage is technically one of the hardest in the sonata. It is materially

BEETHOVEN
Sonatas for Pianoforte

Phrasing and fingering by Harold Craxton

Commentaries by Donald Francis Tovey

1   F minor, Op.2 No.1
2   A major, Op.2 No.2
3   C major, Op.2 No.3
4   E flat major, Op.7
5   C minor, Op.10 No.1
6   F major, Op.10 No.2
7   D major, Op.10 No.3
8   C minor, Op.13 (*Pathétique*)
9   E major, Op.14 No.1
10 G major, Op.14 No.2
11 B flat major, Op.22
12 A flat major, Op.26
13 E flat major, Op.27 No.1
    (quasi fantasia)
14 C sharp minor, Op.27 No.2
    (quasi fantasia) (*Moonlight*)
15 D major, Op.28 (*Pastorale*)

16 G major, Op.31 No.1
17 D minor, Op.31 No.2
18 E flat major, Op.31 No.3
19 G minor, Op.49 No.1
20 G major, Op.49 No.2
21 C major, Op.53 (*Waldstein*)
22 F major, Op.54
23 F minor, Op.57 (*Appassionata*)
24 F sharp major, Op.78
25 G major, Op.79
26 E flat major, Op.81a (*Les adieux*)
27 E minor, Op.90
28 A major, Op.101
29 B flat major, Op.106 (*Hammerklavier*)
30 E major, Op.109
31 A flat major, Op.110
32 C minor, Op.111

THE ASSOCIATED BOARD OF
THE ROYAL SCHOOLS OF MUSIC

SONATA in F minor, Op.57

No pianoforte work of Beethoven has suffered more than the *Sonata Appassionata* from that vile thing deservedly known by the vilely formed name of 'pianistic' tradition. But for a very few doubtful points and for a mystery at the end of the Andante which the autograph astonishingly and completely dispels, the necessary advice for players reduces itself to what should be the unnecessary advice to trust Beethoven and play exactly what he writes. The whole mass of other tradition can be summarily dismissed as commonplace and incorrect. Most of it consists of something much easier than Beethoven's proved intentions. Let us, then, relegate it to a place with the devices of the young lady of Rio who adapted Hummel's tempo to her skill.

Allegro assai

Bar 3 It may surprise some people to hear that Beethoven's directions for the shakes in this movement are absolutely precise and consistent with hardly any exception; so that if we know his rules and principles all editorial interference with the text becomes a nuisance. The rules have been stated elsewhere, as occasion arose, and here it will be convenient to summarise them again with special reference to the present cases.

Bach's rule that shakes begin on the upper note was already nearly obsolete in Mozart's time. A systematic exception had always existed whenever that upper note had just been struck before; and in later styles this contingency happened more often than not. Moreover, a shake at the very beginning of a phrase, or by a downward wide skip, sounds better if it begins on the main note, otherwise the melodic line becomes blurred. Hence the shake beginning on the upper note was crowded out till it became unfamiliar; and so we nearly attain the opposite rule. But now, for precisely the same reason of avoiding a stumbling repetition, shakes would begin on the upper note if the main note had just been struck immediately before. Whatever the composer's notation, you may always be certain that he does not mean a repeated note, nor, unless he expressly writes it, a skip. Thus the following signs

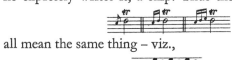

all mean the same thing – viz.,

Nor does it make any difference whether the initials be grace-notes or notes in an ordinary rhythm: whatever their value we may be sure that no classical composer ever intended either

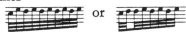

In Op.57 Beethoven often adds a grace-note *below* the shake, as in the examples just given. These cases, then, are obvious. To avoid all possible doubt, let us enumerate them – viz., bb.3, 7, 9, 23, 44, 144, 146.

Secondly, Beethoven does not use the lower grace-note when the r.h. has to share in the chord that supports the shake. In these cases the shake, by reason of its context, will begin on the upper note. This applies to bb.21, 71, 73, 76, 138, 142 and 156. The precedent thus started may

explain the erasure in b.11; and it applies to bb.158 & 160, though the r.h. is unencumbered. This is in accordance with the persistence of dominant harmony and of a strain-upward in these passages. The autograph is extremely clear about the presence or absence of these grace-notes, and there are traces of an erasure in b.11. Now play according to this evidence, striking the initial note of your ornament, whether upper note of trill or lower grace-note, exactly on the beat and together with the underlying chord. Do not break the legato before it. Most players who have acquired the nonsensical habit of letting their trills begin on a note just struck before retain the resulting breach of legato after they have corrected the habit: like the sheep which continue to jump where the bell-wether jumped, though the obstacle has been removed. When your fingers have learnt their freedom in this matter you will find that the colour and harmonic value of each trill is exactly right, and you will be thankful to have learnt the underlying principles, which you can apply to other music, instead of mechanically obeying a dictation which tells you nothing that you can trust as coming from Beethoven himself.

The remaining trills, in bb.44 & 183, are in another category. Neither of them have final turns, as their purpose is to shift to the dominant with an air of having meant that note all the time. In b.183, Beethoven does not feel in the mood for a chromatic F♯ corresponding to the A♮ of b.44. But the grace-notes in bb.184–185 show by contrast that the shake in 183 is to begin on the main note G. The fact is that the whole of b.182 is melodically equivalent to three grace-notes, so that of course the shake will not begin with a skip.

b.15 Players of deserved reputation for musicianship and reverence used, not long ago, to think it necessary to neglect the *pp* at the end of b.16, in fear that it could not be made clear to the public. We may be glad to think that such a precaution is now old-fashioned; and we may be less afraid of a recrudescence of the less respectable fashions of adding *ritardandos* to passages which already delay matters in their own grand style, such as 33–34, 50, etc.

b.51 Never reduce Beethoven's arpeggio themes to their mere outlines. The theme is neither ♩· ♫♫♩· etc., nor ♩ ♪♫♫ but literally the whole boiling of twenty-four semiquavers a bar, until it blazes into tremolo in b.53.

bb.71–78 Do not follow the ugly tradition of making this deeply pathetic supertonic a querulous *forte* or *mezzoforte*. Beethoven's swells and *sf* marks do not raise the passage above the general level of a *piano*: and even this goes beyond the *pp* of the context.

bb.81–90 In both hands the quintoles must exactly fill the beats; and in order that the beats may fall punctually you must train your fingers to mark them as normal accents. This needs attention by the player; but it is a very different thing from accents that attract the attention of the listener. One of the dullest and ugliest misinterpretations that obliterate the real lines of this sonata is the tradition that by hard accents pokes out an obvious design in crotchet arpeggios descending in contrary motion to the theme. Besides being commonplace in itself, this reduces the whole sequence to a dialogue in two-bar

helped by taking the left thumb on the B♮ of the main theme.

bb.142–157 Note that the effect of *sfp* is to keep the first four bars *piano*, and that the next four *forte* bars are marked by *sf* without *p*. Bar 150, of course, then relapses into *piano*, except for its melodic accents in which the accompaniment does not share. In the autograph this passage is written over an indecipherable erased earlier version, yet these points are perfectly clear.

bb.176–211 Beethoven's pedalling exactly defines his rhythm, and the place of his damping-sign at the end of b.211 disposes of the idea that he did not rely upon quick action of the dampers. The unmasking of the low G at 204 by release of the pedal is a stroke of genius. All these points are absolutely unmistakable in the autography.

bb.206–211 All honour to Bülow for his sensitive fingering of the r.h. chords without use of the thumb. In the autograph the C is quite clearly tied as far as the dotted quaver, though this is left untied in most editions.

bb.226–228 Beethoven had bad luck when he used the word *rinforzando*. In the C minor Variations it has reached posterity as *risoluto*. In the *et vitam venturi* of the Mass in D, *sforzato* was printed five times in one page as *scherzando*. And in the present case the perfectly clear *rinforzando* of the autograph has become a *ritardando*, and an *a tempo* has been evolved by necessity two bars later.

bb.301*b* & 303 Emphasise the fact that the *sf* has been shifted to the main beats. But it now concerns the treble more than the bass. A third *sf* in b.305 would spoil the expanding rhythm.

bb.321–352 The fury of these last lines is enhanced, not weakened, if you have the presence of mind and muscle to assert the unaccented dominant chords as well as the tonic. Take the groups that contain dominants definitely in pairs, thus,  and reserve your unbroken downrush for Beethoven's long final pedal.

DONALD FRANCIS TOVEY

Reproduction from the autograph showing Beethoven's abbreviation marks in bb.204 and 209 of the first movement, to which Professor Tovey refers in his notes.

Dedicated to the Count von Brunswick

SONATA
in F minor

BEETHOVEN, Op. 57

20

A.B.254

Andante con moto

Attacca il Allegro

Allegro ma non troppo

[see notes]

Printed in England by Caligraving Limited Thetford Norfolk
A.B. 254

10:91

**The Associated Board of
the Royal Schools of Music
(Publishing) Limited**

14 Bedford Square
London WC1B 3JG

ISBN 1-85472-030-9

9 781854 720306